# Acknowledgements

So listen, I've been working on the book concept since 2016. The first part of the book was created from a 30-day devotional I did for a conference. This was when I attended a church under the leadership of one of the voices that helped shape me, Dr. Matthew Brown. Since then, I mean I literally started and stopped working on this book for years; BUT HEY, it's done now!!!

Big thanks to my Mom (The Real MVP); our Family Thread (LOL, we clown in this thread); my brother; best friends; friends; associates; Dr. Tony Lamair Burks II for making sense of my crazy thoughts; and everyone who has believed in me.

I pray these next 30 Days of Inspiration for Everyday Life, literally will change your life!

# Sets

## Set One
*Days 1 - 10*
*"God Said It"*

## Set Two
*Days 11 - 20*
*"Inspirational Black Voices"*

## Set Three
*Days 21 - 30*
*"I Got Something to Say"*

Scan to View
Inspirational Videos
curated for each day

# Dedication

*To Every *Creative...I Got You!*

*If you have an opionion, you're a creative

© 2021 by Justin Trawick

*No part of this publication may be reproduced, distributed, or transmitted in any form or by any means, including photocopying, recording, or other electronic or mechanical methods, without the prior written permission of the publisher, except in the case of brief quotations embodied in critical reviews and certain other noncommercial uses permitted by copyright law.*

*For permission requests, write to the publisher, Attention: Permissions Coordinator, at hello@iamjaitee.com*

Cover Photograph by Okenna Okpareke of MoreThanOKEY

Cover design by Justraw Creatives

*Scripture quotations marked (NASB) are taken from the New American Standard Bible®, Copyright © 2020 by The Lockman Foundation. Used by permission. All rights reserved. www.lockman.org*

*Scripture quotations marked (NKJV) Scripture taken from the New King James Version®. Copyright © 1982 by Thomas Nelson. Used by permission. All rights reserved.*

*Scripture quotations marked (NLT) are taken from the Holy Bible, New Living Translation, copyright © 2015 by Tyndale House Foundation. Used by permission of Tyndale House Publishers, Carol Stream, Illinois 60188. All rights reserved.*

*Scripture quotations marked (MSG) are taken from THE MESSAGE, copyright © 2018 by Eugene H. Peterson. Used by permission of NavPress, represented by Tyndale House Publishers. All rights reserved.*

Printed and bound in the United States of America

*Wake Up, Be Inspired!: 30 Days of Inspiration for Everyday Life / Jaitee . — 1st ed.*

Paperback - 978-1-954556-79-9
E-Book - 978-1-954556-78-2

# The Inspiration Times

**JAITEE 2021** | **FRONT PAGE**

**30 DAYS OF INSPIRATION FOR EVERYDAY LIFE**

# God Said It

The first ten meditations are grounded in the scriptures from several versions of the Bible, including New American Standard (NASB), New King James Version (NKJV), New Living Translation (NLT), and The Message (MSG). It is through these versions that the word of God is made available to us all. When we pray and meditate, we are able to hear the voice of God. This voice may come to us as silent as lamb or as powerful as a lion. No matter how it comes to us, we would do well to listen to the voice of God.

# God Said It

**Day 1**

*Commit your way to the LORD, Trust also in Him, and He will do it. Psalms 37:5 - (NASB)*

God said He's going to do it! Whoo hoo!! Hip Hip Hooray!! This is the part we get excited about; but, we tend to leave out the first two statements. COMMIT your way to the Lord, TRUST also in Him. These are the prerequisites for God doing it in your life. See, here's the thing, God has already done His part, we just need to make sure we're doing our part. Listen, I get it! Sometimes life will take a toll on you and the enemy will present distractions but you cannot be distracted. Stay committed to the winning plan God has set before you no matter how hard it may get. Have faith in knowing the plan will succeed. Then you will see what God has promised to you, manifest right before your eyes.

**Our Prayer Today**

God, I thank you for the winning plan you've given me. I commit to staying focused today because I know this is the day You have made. I chose to rejoice and be glad in it. I have faith in the plan You've set for my life despite what MAY come my way today. I have the victory, YES, I have the victory! God, You're doing it for me!

# God Said It

**Day 1 Reflections :** *Open space for you to share what's on your mind whether it's now or later...*

To view inspirational videos created for each day, scan the QRs Code or visit, www.iamjaitee.com/wubihome

# God Said It

## Day 2

*But I say, love your enemies! Pray for those who persecute you! Matthew 5:44 (NLT)*

Yep, He said it! LOVE YOUR ENEMIES!! Yea, I know it's a difficult thing to do, but it's worth it! Scripture says, "and they shall know us by our love" (John 13:35) Does your enemy know you by God's love or by your nonchalant attitude? Do they know you for how you speak to them no matter what day it is? Or, do they know you by how you walk right past them as if they never existed?! How do your enemies know you?? You may want to ask them, you'll be surprised. It's important as we are committing to God, we are not allowing our enemies get us off track! Despite what they've done, let it go! It's not worth it! God has loved us in spite of our mess and shadiness to Him! Let's choose to LOVE our enemies despite what they have done or what they may do TODAY. Love them so they can see GOD and not US!!

## Our Prayer Today

LORD, fill every empty area with Your love. I surrender my heart to You so I can forgive the past hurts, the past pains, and the past letdowns. Today is a new day. I chose to love because You loved me even when I didn't love You! Let my life show Your love today. If I slip, Lord, remind me so I can repent, keep moving, and do better on the next test You give me. I love You Lord and thank You for loving me even when I didn't love myself!

# God Said It

***Day 2 Reflections :*** *Open space for you to share what's on your mind whether it's now or later...*

*To view inspirational videos created for each day, scan the QRs Code or visit, www.iamjaitee.com/wubihome*

# God Said It

## Day 3

*I beseech you therefore, brethren, by the mercies of God, that you present your bodies a living sacrifice, holy, acceptable to God, which is your reasonable service. 2 And do not be conformed to this world, but be transformed by the renewing of your mind, that you may prove what is that good and acceptable and perfect will of God. Romans 12:1-2 (NKJV)*

Say it with me, "I AM A TRANSFORMER!" You got that right!! You are a transformer! God has given you the ability to transform what may be trying to conform you! This passage of scripture is so powerful because it lets us know God has given us the power to transform anything that's not like Him! When things around you don't reflect what God has placed on the inside of you; remember, you are a transformer to transform!!!!

## Our Prayer Today

God, I thank You for being great in me! I thank You for being bigger than what's around me. I choose to speak life, joy, and peace to anything that's opposite of who You are in this day! This will be a great day and I choose to use the power of my tongue to transform anything that may try to conform me to the world!

# God Said It

**Day 3 Reflections :** *Open space for you to share what's on your mind whether it's now or later...*

*To view inspirational videos created for each day, scan the QRs Code or visit, www.iamjaitee.com/wubihome*

# God Said It

## Day 4

*Fathers, do not provoke your children to anger by the way you treat them. Rather, bring them up with the discipline and*
*instruction that comes from the Lord. Ephesians 6:4 (NLT)*

This is such an important passage. It underscores the importance of fathers and the significant role they play in bringing up children with discipline and instruction that comes from the Lord. If you take a look at society now, the passage above doesn't seem to be the case. Some of you perhaps didn't grow up with a father and you are holding on to that anger and pain each day. Some fathers were there but left and now you deal with a sense of abandonment. Whatever it may be, today it's time to let go and begin to pray for fathers. This is what God has established for fathers. It means there is still hope: Hope for your father to change, hope for your father to get his act together, and hope for your father to step up his game. There is still hope. So just as you had people hoping and praying for you when you were in sin, have hope and begin to pray for the fathers of the world.

## Our Prayer Today

Lord, thank You for fathers. Thank You for being a great example of a father. We pray for every good, bad, sad, and happy father today. There is still hope for fathers to take their rightful place to guide and lead their children to what You have set before them. We pray people will let go of the hurt and pain so they can look to You to heal and save. There is still hope and we believe change is happening!

## God Said It

**Day 4 Reflections :** *Open space for you to share what's on your mind whether it's now or later...*

*To view inspirational videos created for each day, scan the QRs Code or visit, www.iamjaitee.com/wubihome*

# God Said It

## Day 5

*...But if God himself has taken up residence in your life, you can hardly be thinking more of yourself than of him. Anyone, of course, who has not welcomed this invisible but clearly present God, the Spirit of Christ, won't know what we're talking about. But for you who welcome him, in whom He dwells—even though you still experience all the limitations of sin—you yourself experience life on God's terms. Read: Romans 8:1-11 (MSG)*

OH MY GOD! You mean to tell me, there's a way out?? You mean to tell me the life I'm living, I don't have to live this way??? THANK YOU, JESUS!! Come on and say it out loud, "THANK YOU, JESUS!!!" He has set you free!!!! Yes, YOU!! The one who has sinned, is sinning, and will sin again. God sent His son to die for our sins so He could break the curse of the law and we can live free. What I mean is "free in Him" which is not worrying about what people say, but focusing on what God has to say! You who may be dealing with depression, GOD HAS SET YOU FREE! You who may be dealing with bondage, low self esteem, hurt, or unforgiveness, GOD HAS SET YOU FREE! Do not go another day living in the bondage you've allowed in your life and affairs. Walk in your freedom today!! Not because I say so; but, because GOD Himself has done so and says so over and over JUST FOR YOU!!!!!! This freedom is for YOU!!!! Receive it and walk in it!!!

## Our Prayer Today

FATHER, I thank you for setting me free. I walk in this freedom you've given me proudly and boldly because it's just for me. I forgive the people who I've allowed to hurt me and have control over me! It stops today! I am free, I am free!! I choose to let it all go today. I choose to be who you've called me to be. I take this journey of freedom with a mouth filled with praise and a heart of worship! Today I choose to be FREE!!

# God Said It

**Day 5 Reflections :** *Open space for you to share what's on your mind whether it's now or later...*

# God Said It

## Day 6

*"I knew you before I formed you in your mother's womb. Before you were born I set you apart and appointed you as my prophet to the nations."*
Jeremiah 1:5 (NLT)

Play no games, GOD knows you! Despite what has been said, God knows you! He knows the hairs on your head. He knows what makes you happy and what makes you sad. He knows what you do before you do it. HE KNOWS YOU! So, since He knows you, TRUST HIM more than you trust people!! Ha!! Yes, God! People have to learn you while God already knows you!!! You're looking around for answers when GOD–the answer Himself–has never left you! Turn your trust from people to God! God will never leave you nor forsake you! Choose to trust GOD Today. He's waiting on You!

**Our Prayer Today**

Lord, I choose to trust you. Forgive me for putting more trust in people than you! I ask you to forgive me! Sometimes, the days get rough and times get hard, but I choose to trust you through it all. No matter what may happen today, I choose to TRUST YOU!!

# God Said It

**Day 6 Reflections :** *Open space for you to share what's on your mind whether it's now or later...*

# God Said It

## Day 7

*"Be especially careful when you are trying to be good so that you don't make a performance out of it. It might be good theater, but the God who made you won't be applauding.*
*Read: Matthew 6:1-4 (MSG)*

When you do something for someone else, don't call attention to yourself. You've seen them in action, I'm sure. I call them "playactors" You can find them almost anywhere: treating a prayer meeting on the street corner like a stage, acting compassionate as long as someone is watching, playing to the crowds. They get applause, true, but that's all they get. When you help someone out, don't think about how it looks. Just do it, quietly and unobtrusively. That is the way your God—who conceived you in love, working behind the scenes—helps you out.

"And the Academy Awards goes to [INSERT A PLAYACTOR'S NAME HERE]!" You know you know people like this! People who just want to be seen. Let's not find ourselves doing good just to be seen. Let's find ourselves doing good just to do good. Let's bless others so they can experience the love of God. I challenge you to bless someone today in the eyes of no one. And when they ask you why, say, "Because God loves you."

### Our Prayer Today

God, I pray for those who would rather be seen giving to those in need instead of being seen giving You praise! I pray You show them that isn't what You desire for us to do. When You present us with a situation to bless others, let us remember to do it in a spirit of humility and not SEEN-mility. Amen!

## God Said It

**Day 7 Reflections :** *Open space for you to share what's on your mind whether it's now or later...*

*To view inspirational videos created for each day, scan the QRs Code or visit, www.iamjaitee.com/wubihome*

# God Said It

## Day 08

*20 Don't you see that you can't live however you please, squandering what God paid such a high price for?*
*Read: 1 Corinthians 6:16-20(MSG)*

Ohhhh, this is a good one! I can only imagine what's going through some of your minds!!!!! JESUS!! LOL!! So listen, this scripture said it all! But there's a verse I want to pull out that speaks to me, "Don't you see that you can't live however you please, squandering what God paid such a high price for? You were bought with a price. A high price at that and some of us don't even treat our bodies as such. If some of us were to do an appraisal on our bodies, what would it be?? Think about it. The wear and tear. The stretching and beating. The smoking and drinking. We were bought with such a high price; think about how we've treated ourselves. What's the value now??? Yea it's hitting me hard too! We've allowed so much to come into our lives that we haven't taken care of one of the most valuable items on this earth: YOU!!! CHOOSE TO CHANGE TODAY!!! You are worth it! You were bought with a price, a high price. Start valuing what God thought so much of that He sent His OWN son to DIE for YOU!!

### Our Prayer Today

Lord, FORGIVE ME!!! We played around with a very high-priced item as if it were nothing. Whether it's us drinking, over eating, smoking, or having random sexual encounters, whatever it may have been, forgive me! I'm worth more than I've shown. You've reminded me of my worth and now I choose to act on it today. Better Choices. Better Actions. Better Results.

# God Said It

***Day 8 Reflections :*** *Open space for you to share what's on your mind whether it's now or later...*

*To view inspirational videos created for each day, scan the QRs Code or visit, www.iamjaitee.com/wubihome*

# God Said It

## Day 09

*Beloved, I pray that in all respects you may prosper and be in good health, just as your soul prospers. 3 John 1:2 (NASB)*

Put down the Twinkie!!! LOL! Listen, God wants you to prosper. He also wants you to be in good health. It's that simple! He's given us the tools; but, the question is, "are you using them?" The way has been laid out for us; but, because of options and limited SELF-CONTROL, we tend to fall short! Let's choose to be better and do better. Remember, He wishes for us to be in good health.

### Our Prayer Today

God, I choose to be better today. I choose to be healthy because You want us to be in good health. Show me the areas where I need to maintain self-control. You've given me the ability to have self-control. Holy Spirit, rise up in me and empower me to be in control of what You have given me to control. I choose to be better today. Yes! I choose to be better today!

# God Said It

***Day 9 Reflections :*** *Open space for you to share what's on your mind whether it's now or later...*

# God Said It

**Day 10**

*...Stay clear of silly stories that get dressed up as religion. Exercise daily in God—no spiritual flabbiness, please! Workouts in the gymnasium are useful, but a disciplined life in God is far more so, making you fit both today and forever.* Read: 1 Timothy 4:6-10 MSG

A life of discipline is far greater than workouts in the gymnasium are useful. Whoooooohooo, that's some good teaching right there! See, discipline is something most humans run from! We would rather be stuck in a comfortable mess than in a disciplined life. Discipline brings structure. It sets us up for God to move freely in our lives. Some of you are wanting to see the BIG Miracles in your life; but, God is saying if you can just handle what I've given you and have discipline, you will see what you're needing come to pass!! I've heard my father in the ministry say, "some of you don't need money, some of you need a mentor". See God has set principles up in the world for us to live by and if we can just have discipline to walk them out, we will see His favor and provision overflood our lives. Check yourself today. What needs a discipline makeover? Once you identify it, begin to work on it and see how God will bless you!!!

**Our Prayer Today**

Lord, I've messed up. I've asked for things that don't really need Your working because You've empowered me to be disciplined in that area. I pray You reveal to me the areas in my life that are a mess. Connect me with mentors who can assist me with great knowledge and experience. Self-control, rise up in me and empower me to overcome the mess in my life. Today is a new day of discipline and the last day of mess. I choose to be better.

# God Said It

**Day 10 Reflections :** *Open space for you to share what's on your mind whether it's now or later...*

To view inspirational videos created for each day, scan the QRs Code or visit, www.iamjaitee.com/wubihome

**JAITEE 2021** | **The Inspiration Times** | **FRONT PAGE**

**30 DAYS OF INSPIRATION FOR EVERYDAY LIFE**

# Inspirational Black Voices

*The next ten meditations begin with thoughtful quotations from influential Black voices, from Nobel laureates and media moguls to abolitionists and astronauts, each voice offers us a way to see the world and the presence of God in all we are and in everything we do.*

# Inspirational Black Voices

**Day 11**

*Never be limited by other people's limited imaginations.*
— Dr. Mae Jamison

Ok, so...hear we go: PEOPLE CAN'T SEE WHAT YOU SEE UNTIL YOU SEE IT...My GAWD!!!!! Yep, that's good Jaitee... OK, OK, OK...Back to the quotation..LOL Look here, you cannot expect other people to see what you see if you haven't seen for your own life. People cannot produce in the dark. They need to be able to see and you have the sight. So when people disregard what you saw for your life, don't worry about them. They are in the dark. Just let them continue where they are so when you produce what you saw for your life, THEN they will be able to see!!

**Our Prayer Today**

Lord, I focus on what you've shown me and not what others have seen for me. I remove all self doubt and limited views. I focus on what I've seen for my life today. Today, I SEE GREATER. Today, I SEE BETTER. Today, I MOVE FROM A LIMITED TO A LUCRATIVE IMAGINATION.

--

*Dr. Mae Carol Jemison, an American engineer, physician, and NASA astronaut, became the first Black woman to travel into space when she served as a mission specialist aboard the Space Shuttle Endeavour.*

# Inspirational Black Voices

**Day 11 Reflections :** *Open space for you to share what's on your mind whether it's now or later...*

*To view inspirational videos created for each day, scan the QRs Code or visit, www.iamjaitee.com/wubihome*

# Inspirational Black Voices

**Day 12**

*"Change will not come if we wait for some other person or some other time. We are the ones we've been waiting for. We are the change that we seek."*

— President Barack Obama

Speak, 44, speak!! We are the change we seek. Everything we need, we have built-in to make the change. No, it won't be easy. No, it may be down right difficult; but, we have the ability to make the change. We don't have to wait for somebody to open the door nor wait for somebody to provide the opportunity. We are creative! We're insightful! We're determined! This is what we've been given, so let's make change. Let's be the change we seek.

**Our Prayer Today**

Father, I am the change agent. I can turn bad to good. I have the power to make change through my hands today. I will allow my hands to create change. I will allow my mouth to create the change. I will allow my thoughts to be the change. Lord, don't let me sit in a space that is conducive for repetition. Allow me to be the space that creates effective change. I am the change I seek!

--

Barack Hussein Obama II, an American senator, state senator, author, and attorney, served as the 44th president of the United States becoming the first African-American president of the nation.

# Inspirational Black Voices

***Day 12 Reflections :*** *Open space for you to share what's on your mind whether it's now or later...*

To view inspirational videos created for each day, scan the QRs Code or visit, www.iamjaitee.com/wubihome

# Inspirational Black Voices

**Day 13**

*"Passion is energy. Feel the power that comes from focusing on what excites you."*

— Oprah Winfrey

So the questions really are: "Are you empty?" "Do you want to return to your bed?" "Are you always looking for fulfillment?" Whatever it may be, know that passion fuels productivity. Don't allow the day or somebody's idea hinder you from moving forward. Don't allow somebody's energy to be your source of productivity. You've been given a passion for something and this passion will push you to your purpose. Your passion should excite you. Your passion should light you up. Yea, some days you will find yourself tired; but, remember what's ahead of you! You've been given fuel to push you to it. And this fuel is called passion!

**Our Prayer Today**

Father, you know my fuel level and you know what you've placed inside of me. I speak now that I will continuously move onward and upward. I may fall, I may fail; however, my passion will never run dry. I will have the energy to move forward. I will have energy to produce. I will have energy to make things happen because passion is my fuel. Wherever I am today, regardless of what is happening beyond me, today I activate my passion to press forward on purpose, with purpose, to fulfill my purpose. My passion is all for today. My passion is on for today. My passion is on full, let's move forward.

--

*Oprah Gail Winfrey, an American talk show host, television producer, actress, author, and philanthropist, is best known for The Oprah Winfrey Show, the highest-rated television program of its kind in history. She is North America's first Black multi-billionaire.*

# Inspirational Black Voices

***Day 13 Reflections :*** *Open space for you to share what's on your mind whether it's now or later...*

*To view inspirational videos created for each day, scan the QRs Code or visit, www.iamjaitee.com/wubihome*

# Inspirational Black Voices

## Day 14

*"Start where you are. Use what you have. Do what you can."*
—Arthur Ashe

Arthur Ashe's words are so powerful! A lot of people come to me and they ask, "Where do I start, I have so many ideas!" I always tell them to start with what they can do RIGHT now. Sometimes our fear is fueled by all the things we believe we're going to do. We have to understand we can only get there by taking one step. Use what you have and do what you can. LET ME SAY THAT AGAIN.... USE WHAT YOU HAVE AND DO WHAT YOU CAN! Don't allow statistics and recommendations of others cause you to feel stressed out. What you have is what you can do. Use it! Become disciplined with it and watch what it will produce for you! So instead stressing out, .CHOOSE to do what you can do today and KEEP MOVING FORWARD!

### Our Prayer Today

Today, I'm choosing to move forward. I'm going to be OK with what I have. I'm going to be proud about what I've been given and I'm gonna have all the abilities to do what I can. I will NO longer beat myself up for what's not in me. I will use what I have and take one step forward. Today, I will see what I saw for my life. I'm using what I have to make my life better! Amen!

--

*Arthur Robert Ashe Jr was an American professional tennis player who won three Grand Slam singles titles.*

# Inspirational Black Voices

***Day 14 Reflections :*** *Open space for you to share what's on your mind whether it's now or later...*

# Inspirational Black Voices

## Day 15

*"If you don't like something, change it. If you can't change it, change your attitude. Don't complain."*

— Dr. Maya Angelou

I really second-guessed about using this quotation because it checks the hell out of me! When she said, "Don't complain!" I was saying to myself, "but do you know what I'm dealing with? Do you know what I have to fight? Do you know what's been presented in front of me?" I had to re-read it from the beginning: "If you don't like something, change it. If you can't change it, change your attitude." Listen! I then said to myself, "That's the grown-up response!" I've had to understand there are some things in life that we just can't change. I can't allow that to control me. I have to take control of my life and make it be better for me. I encourage you today, don't allow what you can't do control you. Look within and see how you can make that thing better for you! If not, keep your mouth shut and keep moving LOL .

**Our Prayer Today**

Father, I pray that you give me the patience with the things I can't change. Work on my attitude! Work on my perception so that I can see more than what's present in front of me. Today, I will choose to see better, be better, do better!

--

*Dr. Maya Angelou was an American poet, memoirist, and civil rights activist who published autobiographies, essays, and poetry. Her first autobiography, I Know Why the Caged Bird Sings, brought her international recognition and acclaim.*

# Inspirational Black Voices

**Day 15 Reflections :** *Open space for you to share what's on your mind whether it's now or later...*

To view inspirational videos created for each day, scan the QRs Code or visit, www.iamjaitee.com/wubihome

| 37

# Inspirational Black Voices

## Day 16

*"Many people don't focus enough on execution. If you make a commitment to get something done, you need to follow through on that commitment."*

— Kenneth Chenault

This right here is huge because so many of us have some great ideas; but, we suck at execution. I think it falls with having to take on the responsibility of completing what we will be held accountable for. I really encourage you today to look back at everything you started and did not complete. Ask yourself, "Is this a pattern I want to continue?" Some of you have the ability to go back and start again. Some of you have the ability to pick up where you left off. Whatever it may be, FINISH IT! Don't keep starting and stopping. "WHY?" you may ask: Because you're creating holes for the ones coming behind you. Create a path someone can follow! It's time to grow up and FINISH WHAT YOU STARTED!

### Our Prayer Today

Father, I pray today that you give me the strength to finish. Bring back up the things I stopped and didn't complete, especially those that are vital to my success. Allow me the opportunity to fix some things, rearrange some things, and complete some things so that I can obtain what was promised to me for my life. Today I will begin to FINISH. I'll move forward and complete what I know I have the power to do. Send help. Send strength! I'm finishing this thing! Yep, it's starting today!

--

*Kenneth Irvine Chenault, an American business executive, was the CEO and Chairman of American Express for 17 years. He was the third Black CEO of a Fortune 500 company.*

# Inspirational Black Voices

**Day 16 Reflections :** *Open space for you to share what's on your mind whether it's now or later...*

*To view inspirational videos created for each day, scan the QRs Code or visit, www.iamjaitee.com/wubihome*

| 39

# Inspirational Black Voices

## Day 17

*"If you wake up deciding what you want to give versus what you're going to get, you become a more successful person. In other words, if you want to make money, you have to help someone else make money."*

— Russell Simmons

This quotation is very powerful because it speaks about the title of this inspirational book: WAKE UP. He said, ""If you wake up deciding what you want to give versus what you're going to get," you're going to be successful. I connect that with the principle that I have grown up with, "whatever you sow you shall reap!" Let's be honest, a lot of us would rather get than give or sow. Listen to this, I found the more I gave the more I got and a lot of what I got was more than what I gave. I challenge you today to look at your giving record–and not just financial. How is it like or unlike your getting record? If there is an imbalance, let the imbalance be in what you're giving instead of what you're getting. I know some of you may have been hurt and some people may have taken advantage of you; but, whatever it may be, don't allow your past experiences to hinder your future progress. Trust yourself! Gift wholeheartedly so you can reap abundantly!

**Our Prayer Today**

Father, I am a giver and a receiver. Today, I focus on giving first. I am a giver. I am also a receiver; give me the income and influence so I can bless and gift others today. Amen

--

*Russell Wendell Simmons, is an American entrepreneur, record executive, writer, and film producer. He is chairman and CEO of Rush Communications, co-founder of Def Jam Recordings, and the creator of Phat Farm, Argyleculture, and Tantris clothing lines.*

# Inspirational Black Voices

***Day 17 Reflections :*** *Open space for you to share what's on your mind whether it's now or later...*

*To view inspirational videos created for each day, scan the QRs Code or visit, www.iamjaitee.com/wubihome*

| 41

# Inspirational Black Voices

## Day 18

*"My Vocation is my Vacation. I love what I do."*

— Nick Cannon

This is so dope and simple: my vocation is my vacation. Ask yourself this, "Do you love what you're doing or have you settled for what you're doing? Do you wake up and hate going into your job?" Maybe you dislike who you are or what your life has become. Either way, I say, don't settle for it, change it. You've been given a powerful tool and today we're gonna look at the tool called love. We all have a love for something and that love can and will provide for you. Some of you are great at cooking. Some of you are great at sewing. Whatever it may be, let that love fuel you so your production can produce by your passion. Go on vacation every day you get up because you chose to let your vocation be your vacation.

Our Prayer Today

Father, I pray today that you will open up opportunities for change. Change in my environment. Change in my work life. Change in my relationships. Let it align with what I love. Let it align with what I'm passionate about so I can walk in it and be excited about what I'm doing... every... single....day!

--

*Nicholas Scott Cannon, an American comedian and rapper, has gained notoriety as a television host on Wild 'n Out, America's Got Talent, and The Masked Singer.*

# Inspirational Black Voices

***Day 18 Reflections :*** *Open space for you to share what's on your mind whether it's now or later...*

# Inspirational Black Voices

## Day 19

*Every great dream begins with a dreamer. Always remember, you have within you the strength, the patience, and the passion to reach for the stars to change the world.*
— Harriet Tubman

There's not much I need to say about this one because it was literally in the quotation. "You have what you need on the inside of you." Just watch the video. LOL!

## Our Prayer Today

Father, let it rise up in me! Let everything that's in me that has not been used rise up! The world is waiting on what's inside me! I won't discount what I have. I will walk in assurance that I have what it takes to have a significant impact in the world.

--

Harriet Tubman was an American abolitionist and women's suffrage activist. Enslaved since birth, she escaped and conducted some 13 missions using the Underground Railroad.

# Inspirational Black Voices

***Day 19 Reflections :*** *Open space for you to share what's on your mind whether it's now or later...*

*To view inspirational videos created for each day, scan the QRs Code or visit, www.iamjaitee.com/wubihome*

# Inspirational Black Voices

## Day 20

*I prayed for twenty years but received no answer until I prayed with my legs.*

— Frederick Douglass

Let me tell you something, this quotation right here checked me and encouraged me! Some of you have been praying you've been fasting but you haven't been moving. I'm not gonna get preachy but the Bible says faith without works is dead. Yes, Pray. Yes, Believe. ALSO, make sure you're moving forward to what you've been praying about! If you really believe what you are praying for, you shouldn't be waiting for it to happen before you start moving. You should start moving because you know it's going to happen. THIS is the essence of faith. And all you need is faith the size of a tiny mustard seed!

Our Prayer Today

I will pray and I will move. I will believe and I will move. I believe when I move, I will see you've already moved on my behalf! Today is the day I will see what I prayed for! This is the day!

--

Frederick Douglass, was an American social reformer, abolitionist, orator, writer. He escaped enslavement to become a leader of the abolitionist movement and a statesman.

# Inspirational Black Voices

***Day 20 Reflections :*** *Open space for you to share what's on your mind whether it's now or later...*

*To view inspirational videos created for each day, scan the QRs Code or visit, www.iamjaitee.com/wubihome*

| JAITEE 2021 | **The Inspiration Times** | FRONT PAGE |

**30 DAYS OF INSPIRATION FOR EVERYDAY LIFE**

# I Have Something to Say

The 82nd Psalm declares, "You are gods; you are all children of The Highest!" You've guessed it! The final ten meditations are all from me. I mean, after all, if I am made in the image and likeness of God then I, too, have something to say. And so do you!

# I Got Something To Say

**Day 21**

I wanna start out by speaking to my entrepreneurs and 9-to-5ers

**Newsflash: You can be an entrepreneur AND work a 9-to-5 job! Say it with me, "It's not either/or, it's BOTH/AND!!!**

Despite popular belief, you can be an entrepreneur and still work a 9-to-5 job! So many think you have to quit your job and jump into working your idea full time. WRONG! I worked a 9-to-5 for four years and still worked for my company once I got off work. Yea, I was tired, BUT I knew BILLS had to be paid! See I needed something to fund the Vision and I needed time to figure out a good system for company customer connections. We know the stories on how people went broke and homeless; but, that doesn't have to be you. You can do both until your passion idea begins to overtake your 9-to-5. My advice to you is to make the time and scheduling a priority. Ask yourself, "how can I make this work with the time I'm given?" Also, what's the best system and saving plan you can use SO if you do decide to jump, you at least have a cushion to stand on. The key in all of this is: don't stop working your passion idea. Make your money with your 9-to-5 and then work your passion before, after, or before and after. The choice is yours!

# I Got Something To Say

**Day 21 Reflections :** *Open space for you to share what's on your mind whether it's now or later...*

# I Got Something To Say

**Day 22**

**Faith is preparing for production of your passion, not waiting for your passion to be produced before you start preparing.**

Whew! LISTEN, these words got me together. While encouraging one of my brothers, I said this and had to take a moment to myself. This is what I believe we do soooo many times. We will see what we are capable of doing, sit back, and wait for it to happen. Then wonder why we are overworked, stressed, and having anxiety about what WE believed we were supposed to be doing. That's because when we saw it, we were supposed to start preparing for it, not wait for it to be produced. Yea, I know, it hits you right in the gut. As a result of not preparing, we attract overworking, stress, and anxiety. All of this just to maintain what we were already promised. If we start preparing when we see it, we will have a strategy to maintain our produced passion. Then we won't have to deal with unwanted stress and anxiety. Why? BECAUSE WE WERE PREPARED FOR IT. Don't let another day go by. START PREPARING NOW!

# 𝕴 𝕲𝖔𝖙 𝕾𝖔𝖒𝖊𝖙𝖍𝖎𝖓𝖌 𝕿𝖔 𝕾𝖆𝖞

**Day 22 Reflections :** *Open space for you to share what's on your mind whether it's now or later...*

*To view inspirational videos created for each day, scan the QRs Code or visit, www.iamjaitee.com/wubihome*

# I Got Something To Say

## Day 23

**Ask yourself, "what routine is backing me?"**

In my early years of being an entrepreneur, I found most of my mistakes came because I didn't have a routine. I was trying to go with the flow and thought that was going to get me to my goals faster. Uhhhh, NO! It wasn't until I started my lifestyle apparel–WGSR (Worship, Grind, Sleep, Repeat)–that I realized, "this is what I was missing!" Going after your dreams requires discipline and a winning routine. You want a routine that not only keeps you focused but also provides space for inspiration and rest! Look at your life and ask yourself, "what's my routine? Is it keeping me focused when I wanna look elsewhere? Is it providing space for inspiration? Am I finding rest?" If you need a routine that will bring success, consider WGSR:

WORSHIP - Wake up and spend time with what inspires you!
GRIND - Work / Do what you love every day
SLEEP - Take some time and rest your body and mind
REPEAT - Stay consistent

Give it a try today! It will produce results.

# I Got Something To Say

**Day 23 Reflections :** *Open space for you to share what's on your mind whether it's now or later...*

# I Got Something To Say

**Day 24**

**Being a CREATIVE entrepreneur, one of the hardest things I've found to master is consistency! It's like a car you have to keep starting to get to your destination.**

I've personally had to ask myself...WHY is it so hard to be consistent!??? Well, I want to offer two possible thoughts as to why.

First, there are too many things on our plate. Being creatives, our minds are always going and we're constantly thinking of new things. I've found that just because you think of it doesn't mean you need to do it then! Here's a solution: Write it down and stay focused on what you are currently doing.

Second, you're not really passionate about it! Once I looked at what I was doing, I found that it really wasn't something I wanted to do. Here's a solution: Attach yourself to the thing you are passionate about and give your all to it. When times get tough, you'll find yourself doing what you need to keep it going. WHY? Because you're passionate about it! So I encourage you to take a look at your life and your patterns. Ask yourself, "is there too much on my plate? And am I really passionate about what is currently on my plate?" Don't let inconsistency ruin you; let consistency FUEL you!

# I Got Something To Say

**Day 24 Reflections :** *Open space for you to share what's on your mind whether it's now or later...*

*To view inspirational videos created for each day, scan the QRs Code or visit, www.iamjaitee.com/wubihome*

# I Got Something To Say

**Day 25**

**You will find yourself opening the door to procrastination if you're not surrounding yourself with the things you're passionate about.**

I think this says it all today? Look at your connections: who and what you're connected to and how it looks. What's in you? Allow what's on the inside of you to change what's around you and not the other way around. You've got more influence than you think; USE IT WISELY!

# 𝕴 𝕲𝖔𝖙 𝕾𝖔𝖒𝖊𝖙𝖍𝖎𝖓𝖌 𝕿𝖔 𝕾𝖆𝖞

**Day 25 Reflections :** *Open space for you to share what's on your mind whether it's now or later...*

*To view inspirational videos created for each day, scan the QRs Code or visit, www.iamjaitee.com/wubihome*

## 𝕴 𝕲𝖔𝖙 𝕾𝖔𝖒𝖊𝖙𝖍𝖎𝖓𝖌 𝕿𝖔 𝕾𝖆𝖞

**Day 26**

JUST BECAUSE IT'S BEEN DONE, DOESN'T MEAN YOU STILL CAN'T DO IT! If you don't believe me, Go down the bread aisle....hmph! LOL! LISTEN TO ME: STOP USING THAT EXCUSE!

We are quick to stop pursuing our ideas all because someone has done it or something similar. Let me tell you something, if that was the case, there would be no Wendy's because there was a McDonald's. There would be no Adidas because there was Nike. See, here's the way you make it work: it may be a similar concept; but, you have to ask yourself, "What's MY difference? How can I add my flavor to it?" Wendy's sells burgers just like McDonald's; however, their difference is NEVER FROZEN BEEF in square patties. Here's the thing, there's an audience who loves that concept more than they love Mcdonald's. And guess what, that's who they market too. You have to understand, there's a market waiting on you. They may be doing this or using that right now, it's all good. YOU HAVEN'T LAUNCHED YET and the world is awaiting YOUR contribution. LISTEN, GET OVER YOURSELF AND START IT "RAT" NOW!!! LOL!

# I Got Something To Say

**Day 26 Reflections :** *Open space for you to share what's on your mind whether it's now or later...*

*To view inspirational videos created for each day, scan the QRs Code or visit, www.iamjaitee.com/wubihome*

# I Got Something To Say

**Day 27**

**Faith it, until You Make it!**

I pulled this quotation from @jen.hardie and I believe this is one of the NEEDED tools for building your business and brand. We sometimes strategize and plan so much that we begin to do everything on our own. We then leave no room for FAITH to do its work. I heard @alexmortonmindset say if you are writing your goals and you've been able to plan how you are going to execute them, THEN... You're thinking too SMALL!! Listen, that thing got me too. I'm a strategist, so it is a normal thing for me to come up with a plan on how to execute and accomplish. But after I HEARD THAT, I had to look at my life and ask myself, "how much of my life is planned and how much of my life is FAITH?" Yea, take a look at yourself. Listen, I'm not saying don't plan. What I am saying is this: Leave room for FAITH. Leave room for the thing that's going to scare you. Leave room for the thing that's going to stretch you!! FAITH IT! FAITH IT! FAITH IT!

# I Got Something To Say

**Day 27 Reflections :** *Open space for you to share what's on your mind whether it's now or later...*

*To view inspirational videos created for each day, scan the QRs Code or visit, www.iamjaitee.com/wubihome*

# I Got Something To Say

**Day 28**

**Passion is the fuel for your life**

This is a major nugget for your life. If you feel like you're stuck and life isn't going anywhere, check your PASSION Gauge and see if you're on empty. More than likely you are! My question to you: "When did you STOP believing it was possible? Why did you allow outside voices into your inner thoughts?" The reason you're not happy is because you stopped believing in YOURSELF!!! Get up and start moving. Let your passion fuel you into your destiny. Let your passion be the deciding factor on where you decide to work or what business you need to start. Don't let the year end with your passion "On Empty". Fill yourself with everything that's connected to your passion. So when hard times arise, you can remember: you have somewhere to go and the fuel to get you there!

# I Got Something To Say

**Day 28 Reflections :** *Open space for you to share what's on your mind whether it's now or later...*

*To view inspirational videos created for each day, scan the QRs Code or visit, www.iamjaitee.com/wubihome*

## I Got Something To Say

**Day 29**

### Who's in your circle?

Your circle is an important key to fulfilling your purpose! There's a saying that if you want to see your future, look at your circle of friends. Yea, I know, deep right? LOL But true! Take a good look at what your current FRIENDS and what they're FEEDING YOU every day. No, really think about what you're being fed and ask yourself, "Will you be able to build off of that? Or will you find yourself running to the bathroom?" Yea some of you have great potential; but, your circle doesn't showcase a bright future. If you're the smartest person in your circle, START looking to make some changes TODAY! You want to surround yourself with people who will support you, check you, empower you, correct you, and sometimes not like you but will always love you LOL. You'll catch that later. Don't allow another week to go by and your circle looks nothing like where you know your life is headed. Choose YOU. You've done enough for them. You've literally put your life on hold looking for acceptance. STOP IT! This is the day you choose to do YOU. Say it with me: "My circle will look like my purpose and challenge me to never settle for anything that doesn't PUSH me to GREATNESS!" Again I ask, "Who's in your circle?"

# 𝕴 𝕲ot 𝕾omething 𝕿o 𝕾ay

**Day 29 Reflections :** *Open space for you to share what's on your mind whether it's now or later...*

*To view inspirational videos created for each day, scan the QRs Code or visit, www.iamjaitee.com/wubihome*

# I Got Something To Say

**Day 30**

**Ah, what the HELL! Go for it..**

Do it! Start it! Build it! Make it! Whatever you need to do, GO FOR IT! If you saw it, you can do it! No for real, YOU REALLY CAN! So if you are the hold up to your destiny; don't wait until you get a sign. THIS IS YOUR SIGN! LOL There are so many ideas that you've come up with. So many inventions that you have sitting right in your brain; but because of fear and "NO" you sit and do NOTHING! Change that today! You may not have the money or resources YET, BUT you can start on the plan! TRUST ME, when you begin to make the plan and put fear aside, what you need will FIND YOU! The time is NOW! GO FOR IT!

# I Got Something To Say

**Day 30 Reflections :** *Open space for you to share what's on your mind whether it's now or later...*

To view inspirational videos created for each day, scan the QRs Code or visit, www.iamjaitee.com/wubihome

**The Inspiration Times**

JAITEE 2021 | FRONT PAGE

**30 DAYS OF INSPIRATION FOR EVERYDAY LIFE**

## SPEAKING ENGAGEMENTS

Bring the creative entrepreneur behind Wake Up, Be Inspired! to your organization today! Capable of navigating the complexities of church houses, schools, and corporations, Jaitee is head of his class as an innovative revolutionary millennial. His sermons, talks, conversations, workshops, chats, and keynote speeches are engaging and informative, blending down home humor, age-old wit, and the swagger of the present age.

For more information, contact Bookings at www.iamjaitee.com

## STRATEGY SESSIONS

Jaitee is the creative genesis of Justraw Creatives, a nexus for providing strategy and design for startups and small businesses. The boutique creative digital agency is the parent company of two growing brands: Worship Grind Sleep Repeat and the Church Collection. Ignite your creativity, get unstuck, or jumpstart your work by scheduling a strategy session with Justraw Creatives.

For more information, contact www.justrawcreatives.com

www.ingramcontent.com/pod-product-compliance
Lightning Source LLC
Chambersburg PA
CBHW030058170426
43197CB00010B/1574